Confectionately Yours

TS Hawkins

iUniverse, Inc.
Bloomington

Confectionately Yours
Copyright © 2013 TS Hawkins
First printed by Wordclay May 9, 2009
Cover Design by Kristy Giballa
www.kristygiballa.com

iUniverse books may be ordered through booksellers or by contacting:

iUniverse
1663 Liberty Drive
Bloomington, IN 47403
www.iuniverse.com
1-800-Authors (1-800-288-4677)

ISBN: 978-1-4759-7551-2 (sc)
ISBN: 978-1-4759-7552-9 (e)

Printed in the United States of America

iUniverse rev. date: 2/27/2013

The ring bonding two souls, split one night. One tear symbolizing the death of togetherness| The ring bonding two souls, split one night. One tear symbolizing the death of togetherness| The ring bonding two souls, split one night. One tear symbolizing the death of togetherness| The ring bonding two souls, split one night. One tear symbolizing the death of togetherness| The ring bonding two souls, split one night. One tear symbolizing the death of togetherness| The ring bonding two souls, split one night. One tear symbolizing the death of togetherness| The ring bonding two souls, split one night. One tear symbolizing the death of togetherness| The ring bonding two souls, split one night. One tear symbolizing the death of togetherness| The ring bonding two souls, split one night. One tear symbolizing the death of togetherness| The ring bonding two souls, split one night. One tear symbolizing the

Confectionately Yours

death of togetherness| The ring bonding two souls, split one night. One tear symbolizing the death of togetherness| The ring bonding two souls, split one night. One tear symbolizing the death of togetherness| The ring bonding two souls, split one night. One tear symbolizing the death of togetherness| The ring bonding two souls, split one night. One tear symbolizing the death of togetherness| The ring bonding two souls, split one night. One tear symbolizing the death of togetherness| The ring bonding two souls, split one night. One tear symbolizing the death of togetherness| The ring bonding two souls, split one night. One tear symbolizing the death of togetherness| The ring bonding two souls, split one night. One tear symbolizing the death of togetherness| The ring bonding two souls, split one night. One tear symbolizing the death of togetherness| The ring bonding two souls, split one night. One tear symbolizing the death of togetherness| The ring bonding two souls, split one night. One tear symbolizing the death of togetherness| The ring bonding two souls, split one night. One tear symbolizing the death of togetherness| The ring bonding two souls

OTHER TITLES BY TS HAWKINS

***

Sugar Lumps and Black Eye Blues
Mahogany Nectar
Lil Blæk Book: All the Long Stories Short
The Hotel Haikus
Running Still Water

UPCOMING RELEASES
Black Suga: diary of a troublesome teenager
Poetry Schmo-etry
A Woman Scorned is a Woman Blessed
On My Knees Too Long: Prayers, Proverbs & Poems to GOD
Becoming Saturn: Counting Backwards from 60-30

Books/CDs available for purchase at all major online retailers
&
www.tspoetics.com

Dear Diary:

The risk in exposing uncertainty forces individuals to discuss their differences in hopes to find a common ground.

~Confectionately Yours...

ACKNOWLEDGEMENTS

***

September 21, 2007

January 7, 2009

"As You Like It"

DEDICATION

***

D.E.C.K.K

Nana

EMW

QAS

"240"

JOURNAL OF MOMENTS

***

SPRINGING FORWARD: Chapter Three

SUMMER TIMES: Chapter Four

AUTHOR'S NOTE
Even Sugar Can Be Raw
***

Confectionately Yours focuses on topics such as Jena Six, sexual assault, Proposition Eight, an election, debates, AIDS and Suicide Awareness. Though challenging to merge the various subject matters together, the author was able to document the pitfalls, the successes, and the folly of the lives we live amongst into a journal of moments.

Debut book, **Sugar Lumps and Black Eye Blues**, was the tip of the iceberg in regards to "sweetly" touching upon serious concerns facing the journeys in womanhood. **Confectionately Yours** is the complete opposite! Maintaining a sweet title, the subject matter is unapologetically raw. Each piece highlights a saccharine of truth that pierces through the chaos of humanity. Poetically, this book allows the reader to realize that nothing is concrete as society forces it to be. We are all marionettes, moving to the strings of "normalcy" until "normalcy" no longer satisfies or justifies one's existence.

It is personal. Small secrets were revealed in trying to understand the "power of words". In taking a break from looking through the poetic window, moments were taken to scribble down outbursts, private concerns and elements of self-awareness. Serving as a response to arguments and a mirror to actuality, **Confectionately Yours** is an outline to the next phase of the author's journey.

It is political. Following the campaign trails was a taxing experience. There was an eagerness for the race to conclude, but the continuousness of the media made a thrilling time to monitor the expressions and reactions of the nation. The debates, conventions and media debacles were grounds to explore the political arena in depth.

It is passionate. Each piece is vulnerable; subject to cheers, sneers and jeers. Nonetheless, it is straightforward. Whether speaking on personal issues, political highlights (and lowlights) or just ranting, there lies a quest for answers in civic ignorance.

Enjoy journeying through the Journal of Moments! It is with hope that you will stay along to complete the course as the author prepares to conclude the sugary trilogy with **Mahogany Nectar**!

THE SWEET URGENCY OF ACTIVISM
a note from Kimmika LH Williams-Witherspoon, PhD
***

The second installment in what I'm sure will be a long list of poetic credentials, **Confectionately Yours** by TS Hawkins is not, as the title might mistakenly suggest, a series of "sticky-sweet" verses about love and life. Rather, for those well acquainted with her first book, **Sugar Lumps and Black Eye Blues,** Hawkins' latest work is filled with the pressing urgency of political activism, social awareness and a cry for healthy human interaction. Organized by the days and months of the year when, presumably, the pieces were written, Hawkins' book is filled with a wealth of expression, distinctive style and a plethora of much needed ideas.

Presented in four chapters, in chapter one, <u>Falling Back,</u> the poems compiled in this section present an uncomfortable glimpse of the American political landscape. The poems are "chock-full" of irony and indictment. Here, the poetry is as tightly-packed and unsettling as the headlines in the daily tabloids that continually assault us with words like *9-1-1*; *"HMO's providing crosses and no shields";* and terrorism. Issue-driven, chapter one contains dense, poetic musings condemning rape and rapists; the cause and effect of war; and the myriad of ways that *race* and *racism* is still problematic in American culture.

In chapter two, <u>Winter Breaks,</u> Hawkins takes a calculated look at the rising number of HIV and AIDS in our communities; our oftentimes, life-threatening preoccupation with notions of "body-identity", consumerism and the, sometimes, painful search for the American Dream. Bearing her soul, chapter two, <u>Winter Breaks,</u> offers glimpses into the real-life struggle that the author courageously wages racing through youth and adulthood.

The poems in chapter three, <u>Springing Forward,</u> play with form and verbal dexterity. In this section the versatility in Hawkins' message and in her style come together; and readers will be drawn in by her unique voice. From this section, certainly, *"Cut Out"* will become a favorite.

Chapter four, <u>Summer Times</u> rounds out the book. In this chapter, love, sex and life intersect; but, according to the author, not always *swimmingly*. Because the lighter pieces in the book are few and far between, even though the reader may secretly hope that there will be love, promise and acceptance by the end of <u>Summer Times</u>, Hawkins' resists the temptation to pen poetry about "happy-ever-after"; but instead, suggests that the poem, like life, is always writing itself. If our living is filled with just as many "ups" and "downs", then someone has got to tell the tale. As Hawkins' writes: *"can it ever be just words?"*

A HONEY-GLAZED METAMORPHOSIS
a forward by Keisha L. Johnson, M. Ed
***

Growth is an incredible process. Our external growth is evident and undeniable. However, it is the wonders that occur on the inside that truly leaves one in awe – reveling in the miraculous process that has an outcome that is equivalent to new life.

Nearly eight years ago, I met Hawkins, when she was in her first year at Temple University's Ambler Campus. She approached everything with such enthusiasm. She was an early-work-in-progress; who had an artistic flair and an insatiable need for expression. She moved through her world with a passion and sensitivity that emanated through her very being. It was always clear when she had something say; and in most cases, she would demonstrate creativity in her chosen presentation.

When I first read **Sugar Lumps and Black Eye Blues**, I can remember thinking, "Wow… she really took me back… to *'when grass tickled the toes and hands touched clean sand in sandboxes'"*. It was the opportunity to view her world through her eyes; and to understand the significance of impact and the importance of love that is both given and withheld. I marveled in her ability to capture and contain her experience in a poetic form. She provided everyone with an insight into her life.

Confectionately Yours represents a continuation of life. Hawkins uses this collection as a platform to express her thoughts and feelings about our world and the true depth of impact. Her poetry invades the reader's thoughts presenting the challenge to think beyond one's self; and acknowledge the world on the outside. She goes deeper and instead of telling us about how she feels she has begun to let us know what she thinks.

It has been such a pleasure having a front row seat to her metamorphosis. I have witnessed growth and a transformation that is indisputable. If Hawkins has been slowly unfolding and selectively

and cautiously unveiling, in **Confectionately Yours**, she immerges…
matured, beautiful and ready to spread her wings for the world to see.

MY PEN
a prologue
***

you say my pen is dangerous
that's because you haven't stood in an alleyway at 2am
listening to the gutter wails of a newborn
craving substance from an abused milk duct of silence
starving for everything it can't afford

you say my pen is dangerous
that's because you have never awoken to night terrors of enemy lines
bullet stares of contradiction
cradle rocking denial in slow beating purple hearts
where drum majors rat-a-tat-tat on the fatigued misled

you say my pen is dangerous
that's because you haven't held a conversation with a Black Panther
who sat in the last row
the last seat
where her "by any means necessary"
necessarily meant she was never heard
backpedaling swallowed afterthoughts
her fringe was only decor for the movement

you say my pen is dangerous
that's because you have never been a cancer cell on a suicide mission
holding a one-way ticket to injustice on a body pleading for life
where kitchen sink cocktails are the only in-flight meal
before hitting the towers of mental destruction

you say my pen is dangerous
that's because you never looked a 7 year old in the eyes
saw bright future fade to black on back street promises
where ass-crack and cocaine became pipe dreams of reality
crediting mental math skills to concrete board rooms of lessons
learned
where Red and Blue are still synonymous with shackling freedom,
liberty and justice for none

you say my pen is dangerous
that's because you've never been an untold bedtime story
facts and fables of tales un-rendered to the ears of a 5 year old
who's only wish was to be Daddy's princess
so when reading to her seed she recites battle scars of lost childhood
dreams
birthing militant ignorance of personal inadequacies

you say my pen is dangerous
that's because you've never been a black out drunk
square dancing on table tops
leaving tips of regret and happenstance
inhaling liquor to erase long term memory's betrayal
only to overdose into next week's tribulations
as bartenders continue to pour rounds of mis-turns
mental safety bites the dust

you say my pen is dangerous
that's because you haven't listened to the radio
youth head banging to auto-tune coons
where "lights, camera, flashmob" are CareerBuliders
common sense LinkedIn to spitting rap lyrics on backs of hypothetical
hoes
Supermanning a lifestyle dreams can't afford

you say my pen is dangerous
that's because you have not been the receding hairline of a Black
woman
living out her status quo in Yaki lace-front human remains
stripping her epic memory and stuffing it into a suit that will never fit
weight watching a heavy heart
unable to accept plus sized dreams
reflecting in a mirror of lies
vision forever blinded in trial and error
for the European dynasty shouldn't have been the legacy chased

you say my pen is dangerous
that's because you never watched the last episode of American Band
Stand

the one night the Revolution was televised and integration swept the nation
displaying that prosperity could no longer be deferred
but the FCC pulled the plug on humanity
suppose being an American is true genocide

you say my pen is dangerous
that's because you weren't the last Jew in the shower stall
the last slave dangling for freedom
the last Native Indian receiving a facial full of smallpox
the last Asian at the harbor being docked for death
you just read about it
thinking it was an end of an era
never once pondering that it was a tumultuous beginning to escalating hate

you say my pen is dangerous
that's because the most reckless thing you've done was turn on the news
instead of walking out your front door
YOUR COMMUNITY AWAITS!
I'm only as deep as faucet water if you applaud and toe tap
want my pen to be instrumental
otherwise there is no need to speak
and there is definite dangers in that...

Falling Back

Chapter One

September 11' Political Malarkey

The mind; continually baffled by deceit
Declarations of justice and civility
Written lyrics of harmony created by the hand of a cock
"All men are created equal?"

They are endowed by their Creator with

unalienable rights,

That among these are; life, liberty and the pursuit

of happiness?"

Mismanaged text by revered men
The same leaders that preached change on a Sabbath day
Honored hierarchy during the week
Caramelizing freedom with ink and quill
Enslaving the bronze and the down trodden
From Hancock, Bartlett, Whipple and Thornton
Franklin, Witherspoon, Hart, Penn
To Hoover, Regan, Bush and Clinton
Time will tell
Bold, brazen, and bad business
Will kill your family and make you watch it
Over and over and over again
To prove moot point of unnecessary war
Like an American action flick
Where citizens do their own stunts
Out of buildings that are heaven stories high
Creating a national blockbuster of shame and malice
Titling it with Terrorism
While white washing humanity with syncopated patriotism
"Never Forget 9/11?"

Waving flags to the dishonest wind
Will it ever end?

September 13: Leaving the Nursery

Was born a girl and mama was pleased
For bows and ribbons, no scrapes on knees
Living life of a young woman's dream
Pop, look, reality...

Walking to work
Skipping to school
Jumping rope in the yard
Just following rules
Getting juice from the corner store
Chasing child that's chasing ball across the street
Or on patio to stop flesh melting from the heat
Just following the rules
Rain calls for galoshes and plastic coated coats
Snow, diva all her own, moans for fur to keep warm
Heat demands that meat
Be displayed in a way so sun can play
This were confusion steps in
Viewpoints skewed by temptations
Man-made frustrations created by fabric manipulations
All that can be seen is...

Tank tops on breast tops

Skirts covering kittens

Flip-flops and shell tops

Make short shorts forbidden

Not trying to be sexy

Maintaining a cool

These are a few of the favorite things

That keeps the heat from driving folks insane
Just following the rules
A woman is a lady in whatever she's got
So what if her skirt is too short

All that is happening is the airing of the twat
Should that be punished?
Should that be stopped?
If so, then free balling and pants below the waist
Should be outlawed
If that was truly the case
Attire giving men the right to perspire
In naughty places that need to rinsed out with soap
Mentally groping lady bits
Thoughts triggering physical desire
Yanking, thrusting and lusting for things to transpire
With archaic pick-up lines
Halfhearted compliments
Unwanted touching and rubbing
Pulling away, pulling toward, pulling away, pulling toward
Alleys ways, kitchen floors, street corners, bedrooms and bathrooms
MOVE, GET OFF, STOP, NO...

Verbal restraint unheard
Deed is done
The damage has begun
But he's the one beginning his fun
Jammed it in once
She's paid the price
He wanting to do it twice
Knowing it won't be nice
She's running, scratching and screaming for safety
Can't you hear her?
Why aren't you listening?

All around the morgue you'll see
Girls from the community
A rapist thought it was all in fun
Pop, goes humanity...

September 21 Beacon Defeated

In the blink of an eye
It has come to this
A moment in which wills are tested
Trust is measured about a life in question
America's Next Top Victim
Featuring high fashion abandonment
Couture negligence cascading through seams of commercial empathy
Pronouns reduced to a practitioner's playground of scalpels and plastic gloves
Lovers, sisters, grandparents, and a mother
An entity that carried the burdens of others
Now tortured by the selfishness
Subjected to injections of under staffed facilities
Marinating in fecal's matter while searching for humanity
Medicinal vomit induced slop buckets left to provide comfort
Being strapped down by limply limbs
Life's vision scurrying across tainted floorboards
Success wallowing in misery and despair
Orderlies without orderly conduct
Nursed to sympathy and doctored by ignorance
Insured that health is last on the list of financial priority
Quick to cut and charge with malice
Licensed with criminal intent
To secure their economic security by any means necessary
Terrified at viewing this scene
Trying to interpret what it all means
Watching a pillar of strength conform to a pillar of salt
Bitter mind, contaminated soul and a body wanting to heal
X-raying a mere casket of what was once admirable
Sprouting negativity from latitudinal viewpoint
Never the angle pictured to hear such wisdom
Mind-boggled by the shell eyes are forced to gaze at
Because in one blink
It has come to this
People becoming pen punch numbers
Hospitals hospitalizing souls

Sustaining the disconnect of life
Weakening patient's ambition to believe only medical drivel
Second opinions just as corrupt as the first
Relatives attempting to aid when needed most
Struggling to provide more and realizing that give, can't take no more
Coming to terms with pharmaceutical's outlook
Leaving kinfolk without input
Probes, forceps and sutures galore
Physicians reconstructing foundations without spiritual blueprint
Claiming faith in a position that still labeled "practice"
HMO's providing crosses and no shields
Leaving patients to deal
With false certainty
Can that be called a benefit?
Maintaining the fight to stay in the game
But emotionally maimed
Recognizing, there's no sunshine
If she's gone

October 3: Alleged Hate

Made to eat rat feces, raped and beaten
Expecting adequate answers
Gaining no respect
Annoyed at the system of just;
Needing society to wake up and get a clue
Witnessing what a human never should
If the situation was reversed; discrimination would be the first thing
spewed
Luckily, for Megan, her pigment wasn't the saving kind
Limited are her rights to humanity, as she lay dormant
Infected with stench of neglect
Appalling
Ms. Williams, apologies on behalf of a corrupt
system
Shame you had to bear the brunt of it

October 11: Can Hail Mary Save Me?

I fucked my father
Fucked him so hard
To feel the closeness
That my birth never allowed him to feel
Let his penis be the umbilical cord
To connect the space in our relationship
The first time we fucked
I was in between the sheets
Muddled with doubts
But let uncertainty blanket my ass
As I pumped, humped, stroked into his favor
Inked
Red blotches marked new growing pains
The sheets couldn't hold the passion placed in its possession
Falling captive to his phallic penmanship
Signed away my innocence
As my virginity oozed through his dick
Who could predict the journey was just beginning
Let him bend me over
Doggie styled my way to beg for his affection
Acceptance from years of negligence
Pleaded to him to eat me out
To make room to find myself later in the process
With him I learned the ways of karma sutra
But missionary was his favorite
Submission was the place I learned to find comfort
Strike three
Was at twenty-three
Had me ready to marry an incestuous situation
Could never cum to my senses
Because when we fucked
It was never for me
Thrusting for trusting
Pounding for appeasement
Stroking for freedom

Finding no clarity
Routinely fucking to find a place in the vaginal mind
A moment that could make my clit tick
With pleasure to complete our relationship
But always cumming up dry
Crying won't wet the lips

They remain chapped
As I grasp for his last strokes of humanity
Constantly on my knees
Never having time to pray
Seconds spent suckling for his satisfaction
In hopes to get the same in return
Left to burn
Taking the shaft for his inadequacies
Now looking for closure
It's been two decades since my last confession
Depression has me wanting to start anew

Who knew I would be fucked by every man
In search for my father's presence

November 4 Don't Mean To Offend

If this doesn't pertain to you
Or you don't like what I'm saying
Sit back and just listen to who I am playing
Don't mean to offend
Want you to comprehend
That Blackness isn't a choice
To pick up and drop on a whim

You date a Black man
You bear his children
Believe you're not racist
Because your spouse isn't White
And your one friend is Black
Daily darken the flesh by tanning
Collagen the lips
Implant the breast
Round out the ass to expand the hips
But if…
Someone told you to sit in the back of the bus
You start to remember your privileges
Want all of the benefits and none of the pitfalls
Of what it means
What society deems
As Black

If this doesn't pertain to you
Or you don't like what I'm saying
Sit back and just listen to who I am playing
Don't mean to offend
Want you to comprehend
That Blackness isn't a choice

To pick up and drop on a whim

Stop pretending to be "down"
Mocking afro-centric commonalities
Wearing "Air Fro's"
Garnishing golden locs with cowry shells
Rockin' a dashiki with Prada heels
Assuming you know the Black ideals
Just by taking two African American classes
Trying to blend into the masses
Of being Black, African American, Caribbean
Whatever flavor you fancy
Living in your la-la land of reality
You will never understand the plight of the Black man
On his day off from work wearing a t-shirt, baggy jeans and
Timberlands
No one clutches their purse when you walk down the street
No one is intimidated by your tone of speech
Society assumes you're cultured and well versed
By earning your stripes going to an urban college
Receiving knowledge
And street credit for understanding the underserved

If this doesn't pertain to you
Or you don't like what I'm saying
Sit back and just listen to who I am playing
Don't mean to offend
Want you to comprehend
That Blackness isn't a choice
To pick up and drop on a whim

People of color can't win for losing
When waking up in the morning there's no benefit in choosing
Skin condemned
Riddled and degraded
Slave shipped in your consciousness

Downsized to an afterthought
Will take joy screwing one of them on Monday
Won't dare vote for one on election Tuesday
But give it second thoughts come Wednesday
Because he's a half and half
So he wouldn't have been half bad
Right…
Wrong!
Tired of being the afterthought
While you "Sleep and Eat" the caricatures you create
Tired of remaining black listed
Even when the black face is worn to make you comfortable
Shuck that jive and open your eyes
People are people no matter their weight, color and size
Sick of being bastardized because your ancestors ignorance
The millennium has to bring some type of difference

If this doesn't pertain to you
Or you don't like what I'm saying
Sit back and just listen to who I am playing
Don't mean to offend
Want you to comprehend
That Blackness isn't a choice
To pick up and drop on a whim

November 4: At 11:59pm

Unity
Honesty, Loyalty
Loving, Touching, Lusting
Laughing, Crying, Submitting, Creating
Nuptials

Denied
Unfair, Prejudice
Revulsion, Fleeting, Devaluing
Yearning, Hoping, Praying, Wishing
Matrimony

November 5° Rehabilitation

Taking it one day at a time
To be sober
After yearly shot of political humdrum
Not longing for tonic to clear the toxic of cosmetic democracy
No longer intoxicated with the red whines of regulations
To be clean
Veins pulsating salvation
No longer snorting inadequacies of social order
No longer itching for peace
To be hungry
Consume change in ethical diet
Balancing progress and mandates
To be satisfied
No longer shoving pounds of super nation incivility
Only to purge the past to hate the progress of the future
To quit
Not inhaling racial divides
No longer encasing hope to a nicotine seal
Breathing liberty
Taking it one day at a time

November 11: Toy Soldiers

When Johnny comes marching home again…

He shouldn't have left in the first place
To fight for a President who's not fighting for him
Abusing patriotic will
Forcing armed forces to pillage other countries for nonsense
Dear President,
You aren't worth your salt
People used to be lined up to fight for their country
Women fought for years to battle alongside the men
Now, screwing to screw you and your idiotic decrees
Escaping your clutches because fighting for you is
the ultimate sin
Does it make you feel better that your citizen's
children are doing your dirty work?
While your daughters are not paying their dues to society
As you all sit in the house that's white
Not because it's pure but because it's painted that way
Comfortably answering the question…
"Do you know where your children are?"
Those daughters of yours are snuggled up in their canopy beds
Wrapped in satin and silk sheets
Or getting drunk with their bodyguards
While poor soldiers pray for drunken stupor
In order to drown out the pain and destruction that lurks about them
You get your kicks out of shattering people's lives
While your only war effort is standing behind a podium
Preaching to us the benefits of your destruction
Voting has no justice
Justice for just yours
Manipulated, lost, stolen and miscounted ballots
Political mastermind of international annihilation
But spelling gets you stumped

Honesty has fled your vocabulary
Disgrace has become your middle name
Thus, you constantly trick us to…
Pledge allegiance to ignorance
And the united thoughts individuality
And to the Republicans for which I'm not
One nation under rule
Of stupidity and racism
And justice for one
One kind, one creed, one mind, one deed
Inequality
Using nation's credit card looking for weapons of mass destruction
"Oops, there were none"
Don't worry about finding Osama
Or off shore drilling
Economic bailouts
Nor the kamikazes you call Terrorism
I'm your nightmare
An American
Educated, Black, and with a flare of the pen
Phonically defensive by any means necessary
Catch me if you dare
Be prepared to hand in your two weeks' notice
There's pink slip ready for you to get a clue
Eight years is too long to get rid of you

If Johnny comes marching home again…

Never let him leave
He shouldn't have left in the first place

November 17: After Prop8

The
Ring
Bonding
Two
Souls
Split
One
Night.
One
Tear,
Symbolizing
The
Death
Of
Togetherness.

November 24: 11 Days

A little
Bird once said to be
Careful of people
Don't trust every word or movement
Even if it seems that the story couldn't be made up
Flee their clutches of deceit. It was true today.
Girl tells police that a 6'4" Black man attacked
Her. Pushed her down to the ground and engraved
In her face the letter "B" and demanded that she
Join Obama's team.
Keeping the lie going until the story had no choice but to crumble.
Listening to this made the insides
Melt with revulsion and disgust. Has the
Nation's people stooped that low?
Oh, the tangled weave we've created
People searching for reasons to revoke change; in
Quandary of letting a different creed in to mend fences of the
Racist past that has hindered the development of the
Status quo
There has to be a better way to live
Understanding, it will take time complete the task. Looking for a
Volte-face
When is human kind enough?
Xenophobic, homophobic, passive aggressive and myopic!
You'd think the nation would have learned something by now.
Suppose
Zen is a utopian luxury.

November 28 Lyrically

So, you have a son
That doesn't bother the soul none
Never was a kid person
Felt like Gulliver
Lost in travels when ankle biters come to roam
Too many underfoot
But you changed that with just one look
…at him

So, you have a son
Remembered when you didn't have one
You were fly then, too
Thoughts keep spinning
The heart is grinning
Just pushing
…to get on good terms
By helping him learn
Change a diaper or few
Not just for you
But for him, too
The little tike is cute
He takes after you

So, you have a son
Want us three make we
All of us together
We'll make the stars want to skip
Over the glee that us three make
If the future permits
Let a fourth one permeate
Say that you can picture that
Want a chance to add "step" to the name
Take a chance to step up to the game
The love will be the same

…as before
Before being afraid of change
Before running away from the pain
Before letting you slip away

So, you have a son
That's part of the fun
Making a family
Becoming one
Say it can be so
Willing to try if you are
Just don't let time stray too far

Winter Breaks

Chapter Two

December 2: Strange Gift

She cried
Hollow tears
But not for long
He was wrong
For everything
Last image of her husband resembled a kiss
Like a rose touching a grave
Soft petals caress the tomb of an erased life
Memories and questions unfurl
Catching things he couldn't throw back
Spreading tragedy with every thrust
He promised her loyalty
He promised her truthfulness
He promised her eternity
She lives a broken promise
Faith in him dropped
Like his white blood cell count
He wanted pity
He wanted understanding
He wanted companionship
She could no longer provide
A part of her died inside
After the lies
After the betrayal
After he gave her AIDS
Her strength is contaminated
Soiled all possibilities for rebirth
Re-growth, re-assurance
She struggles
Isolated from friends
Judged by family
Hankered down by new burdens
Memories and questions unfurl
An office rendezvous
Told the truth
He couldn't sustain the deception
On death bed

He pleaded
He cried
He tried to apologize
It was too late
No answers to the questions of *"why"*
But she can't worry
She knows she is next
She must prepare for her own rest
She plans
Doctor bills, funeral arrangements
Colleagues sending their condolences
She's bogged down with constant trips to get pills refilled
…and memories
Wanting to remember the good times
Like bribing son with a cookie to take his first steps
Helping son learn to ride a two-wheeler
Him pretending to be Santa Claus
The romantic dinners
The anniversaries
The *"just because I Love You"* gifts
Holding the second child, for the first time
The family
The unit
The unity
Gone
He was wrong
She cried
Hollow tears
But not for long
His sins
Became her concern
She yearns
To stay well enough for the children
The family he left behind
For an office rendezvous
That led to his death
                              …and soon hers

December 24th "Prop Clause"

'Twas the night before bullshit
And all through The House
The Congress was bitching
About who is a spouse?
And off they wrote
Without a care
To spread fear to citizens
About Gays everywhere!

Tired of the hypocrisy
"The sanctity"
The lies
And the mockery
Choosing what's condemn-able
Commendable
And halfway honorable
Youth having sex before marriage
A baby carriage
A pilgrimage to your sacrilege
Making young hearts false fiancés
Running a political race
Raising kids
Governing a state
Preparing for debate
While teenagers are thrusting two doors down
You look like a clown
Stating *"Every family has their challenges"*
But only for the privileged
Family is what you make it
Two dads…
Two moms…
Step-parents…
Can be guardians too
Who are you to choose?

About who is qualified to raise whom?
Who loves who?
And in the privacy of their own home
Who fucks who?
Fuck you
Celebs get hitched
Then get annulments
As if 55 hours never existed
Cheating spouses
Abuse in married houses
Divorce
Of course
You don't see that as an issue
Married men
Having a girlfriend
With a wife on the side
What pride!
What gall!
What balls!
To spew righteousness in a State of Irony
Yet Gays are the culprit
To the discontentment
To the term matrimony
You have to be kidding
Take your Prop…
And set up shop in the fallacy
Of that spiritual book
In which you overlook the details
Don't preach about what's right and wrong
In homes you know nothing about
You're not The Judge
And even in a supreme case
The Courts have no say
In the way some choose to love
No matter the length of the petition
You have strengthened a community
That would have laid low
If you have minded your business
Do you know where your husband is?

Is your daughter sexing at her boyfriend's crib?
Doesn't your son sell drugs on the corner?
Is your wife giving your neighbor a boner?
Never the wiser
Just a political miser
With your nostrils flared at others doors
Snooping and scoping
Hoping
To bring misery elsewhere
This is a civil case
That will have you wishing
You would have said nothing
In the first place
The torch has been set
This moment you will never forget

Now, Hatred! Now, Loathing!
Now, Disgust and Bigotry,
On, Hypocrite! On, Fraudulent!
Come, Cynical with Stupidity!
To the top of your churches!
And your soap box halls
Judging away, pushing away, and segregating all!

December 25: Bearing Gifts

On the first day of reality, America gave to me...
One noose on The White Tree

On the second day of reality, America gave to me...
Two Towers falling
And one noose on The White Tree

On the third day of reality, America gave to me...
Three Iran missile concerns
Two towers falling
And one noose on The White Tree

On the fourth day of reality, America gave to me...
Four minority president candidates
Three Iran missile concerns
Two towers falling
And one noose on The White Tree

On the fifth day of reality, America gave to me...
Five dollar gas prices
Four minority president candidates
Three Iran missile concerns
Two towers falling
And one noose on The White Tree

On the sixth day of reality, America gave to me...
Six Megan Williams' rapists
Five dollar gas prices
Four minority president candidates
Three Iran missile concerns
Two towers falling
And one noose on The White Tree

On the seventh day of reality, America gave to me...
Seven Supreme Cali Judges
Six Megan Williams' rapists
Five dollar gas prices

Four minority president candidates
Three Iran missile concerns
Two towers falling
And one noose on The White Tree

On eighth day of reality, America gave to me...
Eight years of being Bush-whacked
Seven Supreme Cali Judges
Six Megan Williams' rapists
Five dollar gas prices
Four minority president candidates
Three Iran missile concerns
Two towers falling
And one noose on The White Tree

On the nine day of reality, America gave to me...
Nine troops killed in Afghanistan
Eight years of being Bush-whacked
Seven Supreme Cali Judges
Six Megan Williams' rapists
Five dollar gas prices
Four minority president candidates
Three Iran missile concerns
Two towers falling
And one noose on The White Tree

On the tenth day of reality, America gave to me...
Ten tidbits on plastic Palin
Nine troops killed in Afghanistan
Eight years of being Bush-whacked
Seven Supreme Cali Judges
Six Megan Williams' rapists
Five dollar gas prices
Four minority president candidates
Three Iran missile concerns
Two towers falling
And one noose on The White Tree

On the eleventh day of reality, America gave to me...

Eleven Pakistanis killed by US raid
Ten tidbits on plastic Palin
Nine troops killed in Afghanistan
Eight years of being Bush-whacked
Seven Supreme Cali Judges
Six Megan Williams' rapists
Five dollar gas prices
Four minority president candidates
Three Iran missile concerns
Two towers falling
And one noose on The White Tree

On the twelfth day of reality, America gave to me…
Twelve year olds having liposuction
Eleven Pakistanis killed by US raid
Ten tidbits on plastic Palin
Nine troops killed in Afghanistan
Eight years of being Bush-whacked
Seven Supreme Cali Judges
Six Megan Williams' rapists
Five dollar gas prices
Four minority president candidates
Three Iran missile concerns
Two towers falling
And one noose on The White Tree

December 31 Auction Blocked

Striped innocence
Shaved personal characteristics to mimic accepted reflections
Swallowed poisons of cosmetic wisdom
To shed pounds of dignity
Only to be hung dry due to unmet standards
Remodeled figure to figure out what the figure should look like
Ran miles in unrealistic footsteps
Whipped into shape by doubts
Went under knife to carve away discontentment
To wear painted face of glee
Pigment lightened for lies
Bright; so the world will no longer be afraid of the dark
Flattened the resemblance of cotton fields
Allowing ivory's ignorance to stroke through a history of denial
Shame; can't look at despair's creation
Changed to resemble fallacies of society
Mocked tradition to mime adopted ancestry
Worn, torn and scorned
Discarding cosmetic blueprint
Attempting to outline essence in the blackest of ink
Drowning in self-mutilation
Listen to skin of the woman
Wading in time; hoping
Asking for freedom
Tired of suckling empty utters of social order
Living in waste; deteriorating from neglect
Soaking in elementary teachings
"All Blacks are men"

"All women are White"

Leaving a Black woman to wallow in regret of her existence
Hankering for acceptance
Reconstructing the rightful stance
Embracing the dark, the natural, the exotic, the real
No artificial additives
Still shorthanded by worldly inadequacies
Subjected to crude glances

Judged by color struck lenses
Look at the woman
Tucked away in boxes
Expecting to check off fallacies of identity
Leaving leftovers to be applied to the contentment of segregation
Confined to European commonalities
Where is the beauty in that?

January 1ˢᵗ Nigger

Disrespected
Disappointed
Discontented
At your essential need to be unjust with word choice
Though it's been known to happen
Mostly covertly to mask the reality of racism and bigotry
Those with visible melanin differences
Made to defend
Often times pretend to blend in
As if skin was not an issue
Even subjected to martyrdom of true self
Camouflaging the shell with exaggerated diction
Armed to the tooth with Webster's finest
Spitting lyrical fits around their wit
Spinning in the midst historical ignorance
Making them vomit from their own mental delusions
Lying on a bed of semantics
A scapegoat for undercover hypocrites
Today boldly smacked in the face
In a normal gathering place
A comedy club
Where drinks, food, laughs, and jokes were once shared
But this moment was different
Commonalities interrupted by slander
Ears just happen to gander
The high pitched negativity that shot through the spine
Paralyzing synapses as the vibrations continue
Swarm through the air waiting to be swatted
Lingering pauses crying for justice to be served
Wanting someone to rise
Commit verbal castration to the plebe of moral fiber
Mr. Richards...

What is up with that word?
Negating slang terminology
Or ethnic comfort-ability
It's atrocious

Disgusting
Your need to evoke power
Unnecessary
Prevalent privileges out rank the existence of the race
You constantly berate with hate
You mace in the eyes
Of those clutching the pride
To whom they are
Yet you stand
At a comedy club
Supplying plastic apologies coated the lining of your palm
As handshakes used to cover wrongs
Claiming ignorance in attempt to dodge the media's firing squad
Biding time
Filling in blanks with empty salutations
The stomach wrenches
Wanting to purge the bubbling rage betwixt your brow
All that can be done is frown
Realizing disgrace lies within you

Person:

She is amazingly vivacious
She doubts
She perceives the joy in understanding
She observes the essence of what is
She is the beauty I seek

She imagines for relief
She senses honesty
She strokes the fire of mental passion
She agonizes over the notion of normalcy
She is the beauty I seek

She recognizes manure of the mouth
She utters wisdom
She visualizes peace
She struggles
She expects greatness
She is the beauty I seek

She is amazingly vivacious
She expects respect
She struggles
She visualizes hope
She utters life's lessons
She recognizes selflessness

She is the beauty I seek
She agonizes
She strokes the written language with flare
She senses the needs of others
She imagines for clarity

She is amazingly vivacious
She observes truth's essence
She perceives the splendor of life

She doubts
She is the beauty I seek

Angel:

Death came knocking one night
Pounding to get inside
Demanding access
Tried to ignore the grim reaper
But fell captive to its lies
Wallowing in a puddle of misery
Screaming for chances to be set free
Tired of fighting a losing battle
Arose to turn the knob to let him in
In turning the knob,
A hand of relief
Disguised as a phone call
Touched the shoulder
Halted to answer it
The voice on other end
Calming
But assuring the current fear
…life will remain difficult
When succumbing to moments of distress
Tears rolled down
As if the Nile were the only water source that dwelled within
Continued to stare at the knob
Wanted to control the fate
But the voice on the phone
Kept pulling in another direction
Decided to follow the voice
It was subconsciously trustworthy
Easing from the darkness
The voice snapped reality back into focus
But once again
Death came knocking
Another rendezvous
Dated exclusively
For a while

The first date
A soothing warm bubble bath
Dimmed lighting
Nancy's tunes
Humming through the radio speakers
Crimson trail flowing down the drain
Marks remain
Many moments like this
Frustrated, scared,
Exhausted and lonely
The second date
Took a stroll
Walked slowly off the sidewalk curb
Into the middle of the street
Had a seat
Seconds felt like weeks
Waiting for someone to have the perfect aim
Drowning out the honking
Drivers swearing
The flickering of the red light to green
On looker screams
The cell phone rings
The only tone heard
Pulling the soul back to the sidewalk
Tirelessly weeping
But survived by her grace
She, the voice of salvation
Walks to her own beat
The beads on her head create a rhythm with every footstep
The boom in her voice extends her height so she can reach your soul
A glimpse of her glance will comfort you
Her poems rejuvenate your body
A modern model of wisdom
Biblical testimony
Piercing minds
Filling them with intellect
Fascinated by her poetic prowess
Thin in stature
But has overwhelming power

The thought of her makes sentencing hard to formulate
Just creating images that run together to bleed emotions
She's a survivor's grace
A poetic omnipresence
An unexpected angel

Leader:

Attracted to you
Not in the take you on the couch
Stroke your zone
Make you moan
Even phone home
To tell your partner it's over
Wrap you around stripper pole
Hang you from the ceiling fan
KY on the nightstand
Type of attraction
Talking about the...
Want to get you in the library
With Pablo Neruda on the right
Mark Twain on the left
Nikki G. in the middle of your mind
Nothing but Dewey's decimals guiding the way
Watching you speak is sublime
Constantly lurking the stacks
To catch you chat
About anything and everything
Type of attraction
Aching to be the eyeglass rim
On the brim
Of your nose
Because watching you read
Makes breathing
Quicken
No, not the computer software
Just seduced by your brain activity
Your intellectuality
Makes the cerebral cortex

Secrete…
Well, anything
Trying to hold back
But must attack
That mind of yours
Feeling floored
Lusting after frontal lobes lexicon
Impressed and stressed
To be like you
Embody your knowledge
Strike that
Gorge your knowledge
Like a chubby child to snacks
Inhaling you with fist to mouth
A smorgasbord of smarts
Wishing to bash in you
While sitting in the college desk
You remember…
The third seat from the left
Emptying the mind to be your blank pages
Eager to retain each ink blot
Each pencil mark
Each eraser burn
Even a white out cover up
Just to be covered up
In your educational strip tease
Please…
Your stimuli is enticing
The mind is blown
Feeling grown up
You popped mind's cherry
With your lecture
Formatted novice thought patterns with your poetic scripture
Never had academics taught like that before
Working hard
To graduate on time
To be alumni
Alongside you

January 7: As You Like It

Make God laugh
Display a list
Think it through
Construct plans to follow through
Being canned
Was not in the day's plan
Arose
Cold shower
Pants
Buttoning shirt
Vest
Slip on shoes
Keys
Jacket
Lotion
Shades
Opened umbrella
In route to bus station
Creating mental memos
On break
Go the bank
The post office
Send emails
Grab lunch?
But
Once at work
Rebooted computer
Reviewed forms
Left messages
Had a meeting
Then
Cleaned desk
Jacket
Shades
Grabbed belongings
Left umbrella
Waved goodbye

With head held high
At 12:35
Didn't look back
Couldn't get sad
But being canned
Was not in the day's plan
But made God laugh

January 20' Civic Rebirth

Re-evaluated
The bullshit that drove us forward
The everyday routine
That got you vexed
Caused you stress
But you couldn't live without it
It's the American Dream
They forgot to mention that is more of a rat race
Millions ache to get a slice of the big cheese
Take their cut
Run a muck
Forget the path that got them there
Remembering not to share
The American Dream
They forgot to mention that the cheese is an illusion
A hologram of goals and aspirations
An experiment
A maze with multiple solutions
"But the ones you chose were never right"
Somehow you are always the last one
Needing guidance
Being mocked for asking
For your time to shine
"Should have done it on your own"
Rely on your bootstraps
And when you can't
Quickly labeled inadequate
But we are all marionettes
Strung to move to the lies of society
Waiting our turn
Re-evaluated
Why...
If justice is just
Execution of the process should have been done years ago
There wouldn't have been a need for marches
Rallies

Amendments
Speeches on mountain tops
Burning of bras
Burning of books
Riots
Lynching
Bailouts
Segregation
Genocides
Protests and propositions
But even Pinocchio sold his soul
For a taste of "the dream"
Though he failed, he still succeeded
That's what we call privilege
With new order we are promised change and hope
To share in this advantage
To be equal
For once
Let the four years speak for themselves
For now
Some succumb to the rat
The race
The disgrace of it all
Remain trekking around the track
Looking to break the ribbon for equal opportunity
Eat the destined piece of cheese
Satisfy in the existence of order
Positive progression
Bask in the everyday routine
That gets you vexed
Causes you stress
But you can live with it
America's new dream
Its re-born self-esteem
Pursuit to life
Life of liberty
The happiness of it all
Cutting the strings

Embracing the real lesson
Leaving the sugar shit to the fairies
Creating
"History"
Not his-story
Not her-story
The truth
The truth in change
Let the four years speak for themselves

February 14: Singles Ministry

Wasn't thinking ahead
Fleeing the possibility of longevity
Wading in complicity of naught
Fearful of failure
Completely exhausted by the monotonous dribble
What's soul searching for
If the soul isn't on the list of priorities
Grappling for moments to discharge muzzled thoughts
The emotional death toll rises
Tired of you
Sick of you
At the end of the day
Can't stand you
What seems to be happening?
Melting common sense
While you burn incense
Setting the tone
To stick your penis in this
Can't you understand more than just this?
Tangled in your cake and eating it to
Milk and no cow
Bed with dread
No ring to wed
A commitment unsaid
But a friend with benefits you'll take
That doesn't raise the stakes for you to man up
To take responsibility of emotions other than yours
Won't be able to reach you
If you
Continue to
Abuse the thing we tried to call "us"
The treasure is gone
You depreciated the value
With your licks of self-gratification
Tired of seeing you
Sick of molding you
At the end of the day

Can't stand you
Wasn't thinking ahead
Reconstructing game face
To get a taste of something new
Praying one day that the solo
Can become a duo
Of trust and loyalty
Not looking for the typical
Exotic not a necessity
But won't be shunned
Tired of settling for the almost
Prove to be what needs to be
The soul pines
To escape the single's ministry

February 14 Revisited

Oh!
Damn
Why
We
Always
Gotta
Talk
About
This
Shit.
For
Heaven's
Sake,
Feeling
Left
Out.
No
Dates.
Maybe
I
Have
To
Click
The
Mouse...

February 15 Vague

Love
The gray matter
That combines the black and the white
The black and the white of what really is
And love allows the absence of reality
A story unfolds…

Stood before you, bare
Wanting your words to swaddle me
Comfort me
Adorn my essence
But that didn't happen
Stood before you, bare
The second time
Naked nerves
Muddled muscles
Exposed bone
Aching for your reasoning of love
Giving all that is to give
Allowing confusion to make the uncertain certain
Constantly fantasying the appropriate reactions
The satisfactions of you
Stood before you, bare
The third time
Poked and prodded by your judgments
On auction block for your affection
Blindsided by no direction

A story ends…

Love
The gray matter
That combines the black and the white
The black and the white of what really is
And love allows the absence of reality
But if this is what love feels like
Then hate me
So it will hurt less

February 21 Tainted Soil

You remain alone in the garden
Other plants refuse to grow near you
Cross breed near you
Not as sweet as you think you are
Sure, your vines assimilate that dark forest green
Strong and leafy cascading through your yard
…as well as the neighbors
And on the outside
You are the glossiest fruit ever seen
Tempted to pick you
But you are under developed
Want a fresh crop
Not one who has dibbled and dabbled with the neighbor's banana tree
They say *"you are what you eat"*
Can't possibly consume a fruit
That is only worried about their self-worth
Walk by daily to check your progress
Daily disappointed
Only wish that your essence is as rich as your outside displays
Journeying forward to find purity in another produce
One day you will be fresh for the picking
But now,
You remain alone in the garden

February 26: Repetitious Anarchy Slow Brews (*If My Son Was TrayVon Martin*)

If my son was Trayvon Martin...

He'd be the embryonic melee I crafted from neglecting my past
adorned in media backlash
hood donned in new ghettos
where neighbors watch neighbors gun down peace in candy coated
innocence
complacent to the status quo
my arms the concrete streets you now lay your head
where strangers click "like" at your funeral;
re-tweeting eulogy as symbol of activism

If my son was Trayvon Martin...

The Scottsboro Boys and Emmett Till would have etched told-you-so's
through my uterus
Raping aborted hope from the lining of my womb
reminding me it's not over until the white lady screams

If my son was Trayvon Martin...

X would mark the beginning
the never-ending cycle of debauchery
where tranquility is found in bloodstain blueprints
history;
the skipping American booze record
drowning future in scapegoated fortune
masked in
white noise...
white noise...
white noise...
fades to black
where black fades to the inseam of the mainstream agenda
executing truth to the lies of judge and jury
as "I Am Troy Davis" t-shirts become currency for Oscar Grant and
the misfires of justice
tasing our faces with the same paint used to tell our legacy

lethargy; the paralyses we allow to tap shoe in tar covered pigmented
yesteryear

If my son was Trayvon Martin...
It would be just another Thursday April 4th 1968
assassinated mountaintop hopes
too high for the consciousness of some

If my son was Trayvon Martin...
He'd be the fraternal twin of the Jena Six
that swung like new news until the nation grew tired of hanging its
dirty laundry

If my son was Trayvon Martin...
It means I still live in a world where I failed to do my part
Where Mother Land means mother wounded circumstances
attempt to balance inequities with club parties and commercial
apologies
So until social constructs mean more than updating Facebook
to StumbleUpon a new call to action
I postpone his entry into society
But if it is his turn
I'll name him
I'll name him Aydin Euchynin; God's fiery gift
so you'd never call him HEADLINE
Let him know
that as his mother
its better, I pull the trigger

Springing Forward

Chapter Three

March 15: Nature vs. Nurture

Tussling in titillating pleasure
Assumed the position of
Freedom in self-expression
Submitting to this Love character
For once
A night of passion
Resting
Nesting in plum center
Feeling comfort
It strikes
Wondering why
When ease is pleasing to this current state of mind
It strikes
Biblical teachings of yesteryear
Born a half-breed to this creed
"Matriarch Baptist, Patriarch Catholic"
Bound to never mix
Leaving this child convinced
That the Bible is the attack of mental stability
Tales that circle the brain
Filled with an abundance of loop holes
Most times a form of moral propaganda
Used as lessons and the concrete foundation of humanity
Christianity…
It strikes
This night
The night of passion
First had this way
Had flashbacks appear all day
Adam and Eve
Serpent sagas
Forbidden fruit making mankind damned
The fall of man
All Eve's plan
Banned in this woman's space
It can't be

The routes were so clear
Not sensing foreign territory
No need for internet maps
Or gas station direction mishaps
Simple
Understood by both but the Bible got in the way
Like a marquee
Flashing S-I-N across the cranium
Fighting nurturing practices
Failing in the eyes of righteousness
In refusal to surrender all
The body, soul and spirit
Still battle

Being hammered down by the *"Thou shalt nots"*

Crucified for not repenting
Can't make the mind assume shame
For actions the mind can't view as sinful
Never had a blatant disregard for the commandments
But this one will just have to bite the bullet
Need to feel whole for once
Need to love for once
It can't be
Supposing this is the irony
Made in His likeness
Sent His son to remake righteousness
Hung for causes like this
Free to choose
Yet noosed for dispelling tradition
Won't apologize
Can't let the teachings circumcise the pride
Can't turn the other cheek
Let this Love character in
And now it's a sin
Shut off again
"Damn"

It can't be
Lying in a puddle of self-awareness
Drowning from loneliness

Condemned by the teachings of yesteryear
Challenged to live on in hiding
The Man Upstairs sent His Son to repair
Situations like these
Can't believe
He would want such unhappiness to be
For once
Allowed this Love character to step in
The time was great
But the Bible struck
Changed the luck of the draw
After a night of passion
Forbidden yet sweetly comforting
Compelling and eye opening
But it's a sin to love your own likeness
How convenient

March 30ᵗ Emollient

Woke up this morning
With smile on the face
First time in years
Can remember doing it voluntarily
Usually it's pinched or forced
A plain ol' sour grin
Not searching for change
Content
Most times reactionary from a passerby's diktat
"You're too pretty not to smile"
Or
"What is ailing ya baby"
Never really having a concrete answer
Just direct facial defiance of societal appeasement
Making excuses not to
When handed blessings just to
However wanting the luxury to feel sad sometime
Wanting to mask the daily routine of shuckin' and jivin'
And the painting on the Man-Tan
Just getting tired sometime
Feel like hiding sometime
Just being…
Kind of hurts sometime
But today was the day
To grin from the inside

April 4: King

He had one goal
He questioned authority
He noticed inadequacies in judgments
He witnessed hardship
He had one goal

He played by the rules
He experienced the hard way to life
He handled business
He fretted everyday
He had one goal

He understood reason in the absurdity
He said things he shouldn't have
He dreamed for hope
He tried for peace
He hoped for the better
He had one goal

He had one goal
He hoped he could see it through
He tried to press on despite the lies
He dreamed to dream
He said nothing, sometimes
He understood why that was wrong

He had one goal
He fretted all the time
He handled everything on his shoulders
He experienced the hard way to life
He played by the rules

He had one goal
He witnessed hardship

He noticed inadequacies in judgments
He questioned authority
He had one goal

...and he didn't live to see it through

April 10[:] Conflict

Wanted to vote for you
The opportunity of a lifetime
Make history
Instead of reading about it
Wanting to shout with joy
Of you being the representation
Understanding all the movements
The struggles
The marches
The speeches
Pushing the masculine leeches
Away from the power obtained from war
Looking for peace
Wanted to vote for you
But every time a common ground is found
You switch your game plan
Leaving my voice unheard
Can't let you speak for me
When you swing more than the States that are assigned to
Can't vote for you
If your tune
Is never syncopated with mine

April 26: Mystery in Z Suite

Shock:

Baffled to know that
Friendship is a foreign word
Translation can't save

Phone calls you ignore
Text messages unexplored
Floored at your actions

Protesting the past
Treating you like residue
Yet you do the same

Vexed that you eject
Hate towards them when the mirror
Should be your best friend

Horrible the skin
You live in and judge others
Knowing you need help

Baffled to know that
Friendship is a foreign word
Translation can't save

Spat:

Tried conforming thoughts to a poetic formality
Regulating emotions to a Cinquain
Haiku
Even a Sonnet or two
But I am through
Busting free
No more safe word choice
No remorse for typing this through
After the way you treated me

What gall you have to do the things you do
Disrespect…
Collect the facts before shitting verbal nonsense
Common sense
Would instruct you to check your trap
Stopping flapping your gums out of whack
No calls, not even text
Vexed
From your friendship's disrespect
Perplexed you even call yourself
"Friend"
Indeed your stupidity to the title is tickling
As long as there is a smile and nod
In agreement to your needs
The title holds strong and never treated wrong
But the minute there is slight friction
The validity to the title is ditched
"I was in the hospital, bitch"
And you couldn't take a minute
To set aside your petty shit
To care if I could greet another day
The morning after
Still no response
But online
You find the time to look
On Facebook
Find my name
And happily click
"ADD AS A FRIEND"
Expect it not offend?
Life is not pretend
Nor am I
Going to try
Will not reply
As you did me
One day
As I sat
In an ER waiting room

Without comfort from you
Get a clue
If this is how you your treat friends
Well, on bended knee
On all fours
Ass side up with cheeks parted
Whatever you decree
I plea…
To be your enemy
While I am on the subject
Today completes day three
My phone still needs to ring
A page, a text
Any message of sorts
So I can hear your reasons why
You have not replied
So don't be upset
When this gets published
You had your chance
P.S
This "friendship"…
Demolished
Fed up
Sick of
Tired of
Dealing with you

Reconcile:

Rolling on the floor
Laughing my head off because
You're mediocre

Wished for decency
From you, but given the worst
Never treated you

Like that and this spat
A dumb one at that has changed
A revered bond; sad

To think you're different
Just like the others you preach
About and surprised

Surprised at me, thought
Your intentions were the best
Should invest better

Rolling on the floor
Laughing my head off because
You're mediocre

May 11: Aftermath of Fertilization

Father, take a moment to shush
Let my Mother speak please
Let my Mother speak please
Can't hear her cries
Over your screaming

You're stinging from his salt grain empathy
The pain and strain is evident
Another reason not to give birth to me

Continuous verbal pounding on embryonic life
These pessimistic vibrations serving as staccato astringents
You're stinging from his salt grain empathy

Feeling the weight of your relationship strife
Plot the departure; you're emotionally dormant
Another reason not to give birth to me

Incubating me, hording me, using me to make you the housewife
Fight, take a stand against this man; this tyrant
You're stinging from his salt grain empathy

Claim your goals, mold your soul; take control of your life
Want to be an incandescent gift; not an ailment
Another reason not to give birth to me

His guilt is consuming your life
Your pain and strain is evident
You're stinging from his salt grain empathy
Another reason not to give birth to me

Father, take a moment to shush
Let my Mother speak please
Let my Mother speak please

Can't hear her cries
Over your screaming

May 21 Elevation vs. Degradation

Raised you before you were ready
Set in stone visions of perfection
Letting theory fog reality
Concretely forming delusions of your humanity
Each pathway an illusion of prominence
That you held high
Until the stakes matched that level
Heeded every word formulated
Followed the advice
Stood your ground
Wore gossip's crowned thorns
Respecting your existence
Only for you to stop treating me the same
Can it really be a dance we do
When the focal point changes
With new un-comfortability
Exhausted
Erasing the nexus to mortal essence
You lived up the tribute until you wanted to feel again
Constantly ruining my attempt to excellence
Creating new statues of limitations to suit you
Nonsense
Stand firm
Quit straddling the middle ground
What more needs to be done
Starving from the lack of attention
Becoming malnourished from sipping sieved wisdom
Not a jigga boo
That's content with a master's residue
You asked for this pedestal
Built it for you
Only to be shoved under pendulum
You are the bottom feeder
With humility falling to zero
Below the meter
Never was supposed to end up here
Running out of gas

Prefer surviving on empty
Than pay full price
For the misconception of you

May 23: Cut Out

Time. Time and again. Stumble. Not knowing where falling. Fell. Not being caught. *"Damn, won't do that again"*. But time. Time and again. Stumble.

Lesson. The soul search. Not on the outline. Made to understand the unwritten word. Confused. Yet, stumbling. Still falling. Time, time and again. No net to catch the pain. Cry. Hot melting tears of suffering. Can't erase the throbbing. That's life.

Sing. Sing on to ease the pain. *"Off key you say. Trying, damn you"*. Sing on. Continuously. To drown out sorrows that cloud sanity. Being crazy, okay. But insanity not acceptable. Sing on. Continuously. The lesson. The soul search. Confusion. Not knowing where falling. Fell. Time, time and again.

Catch. Grasping for slippery hands. Wet hands. Abandoned by hands. All hands. The only way out. No grip. Fell. Not knowing where. To yearn. Salvation leaks from the oily palms. No support. Voice unheard. Yelling to muted ears. Each time. Time, time and again. Not knowing where falling. Fell.

Discarded. Time, time and again. Self-comfort can't heal wounds. Without strength, powerless. *"Don't do it they say"*…*"you don't know how it feels"*. No one listens. Their decision. Each time. Time, time and again. Not knowing where falling. Fell.

Gulp. The breath. The last. Unknown hands reaching for lifeless life. Too, late to sustain. Cries unheard. The accident. Reached out. No nets to catch the pain. The wrists, they bleed. Knives secure comfort. Splitting flesh. A piece leaves peace. None available before. *"Told them so"*. No one listened. Deaf to warning signs. Each time. Not knowing where falling. Fell. Gulp. The last. Breath.

Summer Times

Chapter Four

June 6ᵗ Six (*a rapist perspective*)

Take a deep look at this place
While I slip hands right down your waist
Push your hips down to the floor
I'm your mirror, don't grab that door
I need you inside of me
Sinners needing time to breathe
Just two souls about to break
Come on and complete me

Feeling like a beast on retreat
She's not yelling or giving a shriek
But her eyes are rambling a mile a minute
Searching for the letter formations
That her lips won't dare part to say
Guiding her body with her own fear
Looking to flee
With every turn she sees me
Her ubiquitous nightmare
The hunt has begun
With me, the owl
She, my field mouse
Scurrying across bed sheets
Attempting to trounce predator with non-verbal restraint
Biting, pinching, kicking and squirming
Words are useless in the dark of night
She knows this…

Just face it
It's not about you
Quit the charade
Pillows can't serve as a barricade
Finally getting my way
Time to swoop down on prey
Won't hurt you

Because it's not about you

Not trying to make you sweat
This thrust is not to make you wet
Just let me pet your clit
Lick your tit
Spread your lips so my dick
Can slit what you claim as virtue
Won't hurt you
Just remember it's not about you
With this moment I survive
Nourishment in this hungry world
Of pride, acceptance and success
None of which I was awarded
Until this moment

Feeling like a beast on retreat
Getting the way my hand should have been dealt
Basking in what glory felt
With this sexual game we play
Lying across your moist flesh
Stroking hands through every meaty crevice
Giggling as you tug, yank and pull me away
Because you're failing
And I am not
The body has melted into what I am serving
I cloy your senses
Sinner's confluence
Bodies and souls intertwine with each angry moan
Makes me triumphant
With forceful obedience
Someone's listening to me…
You're listening to me…

I need you inside of me
Sinners needing time to breathe
Just two souls about to break

Come on and...
Come on and...
Cum
Complete me

June 15: Summer Blues

Juvenile; mindless hogwash
Equals clouded fluffy thoughts of love
See, young hearts burn quick
Under the flames of a dick with no conscious
Another one bites the dust
As her attention shifts from majoring in academics
To minoring in a major situation
She forgot that she was 17
And he 33
She thought her parents were mean
With college preparations
Forcing financial aid papers down her throat
College tours and career decisions
But nothing is painstakingly difficult as standing in a welfare line
With a child on the way
Before…
She focused on losing five pounds to fit designer jeans
And gossiping on favorite sitcom scenes
Now…
She just worries
Lost her pride
Lost her stride
Lost her guy
And for a brief moment
Lost the will to live
The need to strive
He took flight
Continuing his life
He never meant to stay
Played the game long enough
To touch down on her
Field his needs
…and now
She's held back
With no one to hold her up
When focus is lost
Juvenile mindless dribble forms

From the tongues of the ones
…that need guidance
But the kind given
Is not needed
It's forbidden
She 17
He 33
He should have known better
She, a minor in a major situation
He, her mentor
Left her high and dry
With no explanation as to why

June 27: Lavender

Fragrant
Poignant smell
Pierces
Lingers
Sends triggers
Senses overloaded
Exploded
With the notions of you
Falling
Backwards
Forwards
And In
Admiration
Fascination
Attraction
Spawns fornication
An exploration
To tend your garden
Field your needs
Nurture your soil
Be your breeding post
Lured by you
The fragrance
Penetrates
Stems ejaculate
Feelings hesitate
To admit
Anything
Addicted
Splendid
Connected
To the aroma
Of you

July 4⁴ Passport

Forgive me
For not being patriotic
I do not
Pledge allegiances
To a flag
That has United States of duplicity
Where freedom had to be fought for
By any means necessary
From settlers that stole an existing existence
Serving smallpox alongside maze
And tragic mulattos with collard greens
While wearing dashikis, moccasins and draped cotton laced linens
To think that was only the beginning
Land conceived of guilt and fear
Of knowing that the minority
Will soon learn they are the majority
Hold them down
Won't teach them to read or write
But teach them to recite biblical doctrine
To hate themselves
Or throw a casino their way
As pay day for already claimed land
The plan all along to find something that was never lost
And honor it in history's text
You can't take credit for freeing the free
You can't take credit for writing deceit
Spewing it on a taxpayers dime
Under the codes of FICA-M
FICA-R
For some CH-SUP
And PA-EDU
What a crime
So forgive me
For not being patriotic

The Red, White and Blue
Is the voodoo that you do
Can't get caught up in your spell
Don't really care
About the rockets' red glare
Honoring warfare on the backs of shame
Refuse to be the All-American goof
Saluting troops
To fight the unexplained
Pillage foreign lands
When this place some call home
Is sinking in the sands desolation
So forgive me
For not being patriotic
Can't shout "Yes We Can"
When they still won't
Vote for the colored vote
To a billed right
Instead an amended amendment
Have a deep gripe
With those alleged Stars and Stripes
Forever, taxation without representation
The Government spends half the check
Half surviving
Suppose that is the luxury of the middle class
Where is the voice of the people?
Vice Presidents live in public housing
When half the public lives on the streets
Or living off the streets
Because Arts and Education are the first to go
When the budget is low
Leaving neighborhood children
Strapping up
To earn a buck
To fill the family's gut
So much hustling gets them caught up
Growing up, before their time
Doing time

For just getting by
But for hunting fun
Cheney misuses his gun
His slate
Shoved under the rug
Wiped clean
Yet, T.I. has 45 days to redemption
With Mr. Phelps trailing behind
So forgive me
For not being patriotic
The honeymoon period is over
For some it never begun
Could never say "I Do"
To the same sex
Because the Church and State
Decided to fornicate laws after their separation
In The Courts they dispute

Evolution versus Creation

Jesus versus Nostradamus

Noah with his Ark

Attempts to out serve the golden arches

All religious money markets
Supersizing the Pride of a nation
Taking the time to sign the dotted line
That being Gay is an abomination
Surprised you could find the time
With Priests preying on altar boys
Nuns loving each other
Instead of the Holy one's Son
Christian churches with private CD's
Investing investments in personal gain
Begging for more in the collection plate
Leaving the spiritual community maimed
And homosexuality is the blame
Stay in your lane
As the first official divorce
…under God

You should put down your stones
The glass House is a bit unguarded
So forgive me
For not being patriotic

July 15: Casting Types

Living in middle ground
Trying to live off the beats and sounds
Recognizing it's not enough
There's got to be more
Sick of a labor liquored bore
Work and no play
Night fusing with day
Grasping for another way
Over working to keep you at bay
And wishing you'd get the point
Paychecks benchmarking professional prospects
Never having time for self
Can't cash-in on a rational vacation hospice
Because you would want to follow
Feeling hollow
Wallets gleam joyfully
Heart's beating remorsefully
Miserable
Need something new
Running into the same screen play
Different actors, same writers
Type casting the same issues
Wanting change
Receiving the mundane
Stressing over rocks and hard places
Crooning and swooning other ideals
Being swept up in what's normal
Forced to place square peg in matching hole
Why can't the circle one fit?
Need it; to be the solution
Though a proctor's nightmare of situational structure
Desperately needing something new
Spoon-fed negativity
For looking outside the box
Attempted a quest for a love interest
Inside a time clock
No luck

Primped and poised
Etiquette-ly trained
Real urges slain
To remain prepared for you
Don't want you
Every day and night
Forced to look out for you
Look at you
Look to you
Can't be for you
Wasn't wired that way
Overstayed
The invitation to your consciousness
Don't want to be together
Just because the anatomy fits

July 20: Work, or Change

The last time I orgasmed...
Was the last...
Lived a release-less existence
In order to cum to my senses
Sip on rum
Vodka
Tequila
Shot of scotch or two
And a beer for character
In hopes to have night fly by
Await the alarm clock
To wake me from the drunken haze
Glaze over morning routine
To identify self
Within the confines of an overloaded workplace
Killed by the sword of work ethic
Started by maiming dignity
Elevated tambour to sound non-treating
Lightened the vocabulary to reach their level of understanding
Permed ebony locks
Replaced the black and green
With blue and white
To accommodate the red
Pledged to forget myself in the process to move up in the company
Only to be terminated for following "policy and procedure"
The new bitch
Intimidated that the underling knew more
Vexed that I was autonomous
Educated to outwit the bullshit
She tried to masquerade as common sense
Pissed the black chic
Wasn't the "black chick" she read about in news picks
The bitch
Viewed me as the tar baby that needed to know her place
Though she mastered knowledge
I crafted a niche
That outweighed her parchment mask of intelligence

Killed by the sword of work ethic
In order to cum to my senses
Sip on rum
Vodka
Tequila
Shot of scotch or two
And a beer for character
In hopes to have night fly by
Await the alarm clock
To wake me from the drunken haze
Glaze over morning routine
To identify self
Within the confines of an overloaded workplace
Lesson learned
Feelings hurt
Work's passion not burned
But hard to wake up in the morning
When a beer defines your character
Because everything was sacrificed
For a company that cared less
Cared less about the hard work
Cared less about teamwork, cared less
Just wanted to cause stress
"I won't be the pawn

On your chess board

Of corruption"
So the bitch
Created drama to get rid of me
My complexion seemed to be the complexity of the situation
Bowed out gracefully to contain last moments of dignity
Giving her a false security of victory
Despite my last acts of humanity
Realization steps in
The last time I orgasmed...
Was the last...
Lived a release-less existence
Until this poem

August 8: Ballad of the Seasons

Summertime and livin' is easy
No wounds to bear, no tears to cry
I wear a smile, no need to frown now
So blessed, nothing to weigh me down

There is passion in truth

Wintertime and lovin' is easy
No tears to cry, being treated right
I'm not rich but I wear a smile now
So blessed, nothing to weigh me down

There is blessing after trial

Springtime and laughin' is easy
Feel so good, like a woman should
Found my way, up from the ground now
So blessed, nothing to weigh me down

There is a victory in release

Summertime and livin' is easy
No wounds to bear, no tears to cry
I wear a smile, no need to frown now
So blessed, nothing to weigh me down

August 28: New Meaning

You are unworthy
You wonder why we hate what you stand for
You hear the gossip that you've created
You see the destruction of your actions
You are Jena's memory

You pretend stand tall amidst chaos
You feel stronger than your exterior displays
You touch our youth
You worry when beneficial to your character
You are unworthy

You understand nothing
You say nothing
You dream nothing
You try to confuse
You hope no one sees your symbol of wisdom crumbling
You are Jena's memory

You are not brave
You hope to play the part
You try to hinder others
You say nothing
You understand that your timber is corrupt

You are unworthy
You worry your roots will rot exposing truth
You touch our youth
You feel convinced as a vessel of knowledge
You pretend to bare the fruit of clarity

You are Jena's memory
You see the destruction of your actions
You hear the gossip that you've created
You wonder why we hate what you stand for
You are unworthy
You are that symbol of ignorance

You are the display of hopelessness
You are the plague of racism
You are unworthy to be a tree

August 31˙ Just Words

Can it ever be just words?
Squiggles and squirmy lines
Bending to break the silence
No, those bold formations
Hold a power
Try to contain them in syntax
Train them with the soft palette
Break them down
Sound by sound
Try to beat them
Over throw their reign
And being defeated
Joined them
By hiding behind them
Becoming a parchment gazer
Demoted to pushing the tab button
Letting them flood in
Making the non-tangible attainable,
Somewhat meaningful
A voice itching for worth
Validation
Cringing at the challenge
To be different
With the same lingual blueprint of the masses
"Constants and vowels aren't to be messed with"
Pressing on keys
Receiving letter formation
That covers the page
But creeping behind spell check
Finding ownership with the dictionary
Pillowing the blows with the thesaurus
Imitating editing
Succumbing
Letting them speak

Can it ever be just words?

The ones in use
Are not owned
On loan
The words
On the page
Agreeing with their research
But hiding
Not taking ownership with their truth
No truce
Erasing the lettering
Staring at vacant space
Pressing the tab button
Stroking the keyboard
Deciding to highlight the empty page
Because that's the final thought
The truth does hurt
Not mature enough to defend it
Understanding
It can never be just words

HOMESCHOOLED
an epilogue
***

you don't want my living room to be a classroom
I will teach my kids that eco-friendly
means giving green cards to your enemies
provide new declaration to terroristic threat
Hitler heil down your door
draft whore your sons
to your daughter's maiden head ideologies of revenge

you don't want my living room to be a classroom
I'd bring back the Salem Witch trials
for those seldom trial-ed white collared button downs
stake burn their souls in writ book blaze night skies
under twinkling demise
birth heirs of Tichiba
while conjuring potions in the lost art of honesty

you don't want my living room to be a classroom
in P.E
I'd teach them aviation
to be the next nation of airline sophistication
fly straight through your skull
allow mental menstruation
to leak reality down your forethoughts

you don't want my living room to be a classroom
I'd use Sex Ed.
as a political hot bed of deadhead tactics
fucking every bowel twisted lie with maniacal fudgery
where being anal retentive gets you ass jabbed by humanity

you don't want my living room to be a classroom
history will become "his story" finger raped by rectitude's misery
parched parchment draped in blood stain molasses
while repetitious anarchy slow brews
sin sipped through embryonic teacups

juxtaposed pinky up
saddle bagging high noon
twelve paces back to the moment where the forefathers
should've been held at gun point to pen the truth

you don't want my living room to be a classroom
I'd take civility wedged up the flag pole
salute against status quo
for your safety
you want my kid to be the cookie cutter
passport carrying
"America the Beautiful" soothsayer
so by all means, please
concede to the one you call faggot
the flat-backing unmarried miscreant
the porn star
the bigot
the pedophile
to teach my child
despite what you deem as their flaws
they're bound by law
to spew the standardized fabrications
you call 'education'

THE HAWKIAN STYLE
an afterward by Jason Del Gandio, PhD
author of *Rhetoric for Radicals: A Handbook for 21ˢᵗ Century Activists*
www.jasondelgandio.com
***

I am feeling compelled to be as honest as the author has been in the preceding pages.

TS Hawkins and I know each other personally, having been friends for the past few years. Her laugh, smile, humor, quick wittedness, public persona, kindness, supportive nature, as well as her poetic and thespian abilities make her a wonderful friend. Despite our friendship, I was a bit surprised when she asked me to write this Afterward. "Oh, wow. Yeah, sure; I'd be happy to," I said. While flattered, I was also anxious. What if the poems don't speak to me? What if I am forced to negotiate this professional obligation with our interpersonal relationship? What if, in all honesty, I don't like the book? I am glad to say that my hesitancy was undoubtedly premature. I am proud of her and feel honored to provide readers with some concluding thoughts on **Confectionately Yours**!

Confectionately Yours is a courageous work detailing the existential dilemmas of the human condition. It begins with her personal positioning in the world. How she sees, how she feels, how she thinks, and how she loves, hates, dreams, and desires. It speaks from her politics, her experience, her womanhood, her worldview. However, **Confectionately Yours** does not dwell within the personal, only. No. It moves *through* the personal into the collective experience of what it means to be a human being. The struggle, loss, confusion, peaks and valleys, laughs, winces, giggles, sex, and tears. These are the things of human flesh. Our bodies are concrete masses of ongoing experience, always there: just *there*, always. Because of that, the world can seem like a stable, consistent place. We wake up, have our coffee, shower, jaunt through the daily schedule, stub a toe or two, catch a flirtatious and flattering wink from a few, and poof, the day is done! But our bodies sometimes encounter uncertain moments, unforeseen circumstances, and, unfortunately, unwanted experiences.

These moments then jump out; making us brutally aware that being human is not always a consistent stream of stability. Suddenly losing a loved one, being fired for no good reason, being sexually assaulted, questioning one's faith, losing your passion for your partner, falling in love all over again, waking puffy eyed from a glorious one night fling, grasping the dark underside of American history, feeling hopeful yet skeptical of new political leadership, and confronting the fears and joys of everyday living. We can choose to ignore these inconsistencies and instabilities and attend to more "practical matters," like making coffee and following our schedules. Alternatively, we can choose to embrace these ups and downs and live with them, understand them (at least in part), and express them with poetic passion and craft. This latter choice is the work of **Confectionately Yours**. It brings us face-to-face with experiences that are both unique and universal, allowing us to simultaneously question and embrace ourselves, each other, and our shared social world.

As some readers may know, **Confectionately Yours** is her second book of poems. The first, **Sugar Lumps and Black Eye Blues**, chronicle's, among other things, the author's many relationships throughout the years. Parents, friends, teachers, God, herself, romantic partners, unsolicited partners, first timers, long timers, those who are gone, those who are still here, and mere subway acquaintances. That earlier book, as well as the current, displays her penchant for poetic rhyme and rhythm. The breath, the pause, the quick and slow, stop and go, line break; linking it all together in ways that you can read *and* hear. That's the "Hawkian-style" coming through, and it works in every instance. When reading the books back-to-back you get the sense that this is an author who has grown; an author who has used the experience and insight of the first to expand and advance in the second. That is true not simply as a writer, but also, and perhaps more importantly, as a person moving through the world. She is willing and wanting to learn as she goes, flowing with the winds at her back and growing with the grounds beneath her feet. It is only a matter of time before we are graced with her next work, tentatively titled **Mahogany Nectar: a Poetic Memoir**. I am looking forward to reading/hearing that voice again and to learning of her newest journeys and insights. I want to learn more about her, her politics, her worldview, and about the trials and tribulations of being human in a perpetually changing and challenging world. But for now, I am more than delighted to dwell within the honesty, courage, and existential truthfulness of **Confectionately Yours**.

SNEEK PEAK
***
an excerpt from "Mahogany Nectar"

Highlighting the good, the bad, the ugly and the hilarity of twenty some years **Mahogany Nectar** takes you to the initial stages that forged a bond between the author, the pen and the written word. She speaks about a broken home, a loving mother, a puzzle-piece lineage, woes of the collegiate life, proms and promenades, death, rebirths, sexuality lessons at the neighborhood park and community pool. Although the bookend to the saccharine glazed trilogy, sharing these experiences is only the beginning!

Heaven's Little Girls (excerpt)

Little girls dream
Dream of adulthood
Dream of princes to save the day
Dream of wedding bells
Never that girl
Had a He-Man bedspread
Until Mama said to be more girly
Replaced by Strawberry Shortcake
With complimentary Tinkerbelle hygiene products
Ruffled socks and a thousand shades of pink…
…little girls dream
Dream of ponies
Dream of wearing make-up before high school
Dream of being a lady
Played the part
For some years now…
Maintained an image
Ultimately, hiding
Could never be "that girl"
No matter how hard the trying
Realizing that's okay
For the first time…

ABOUT THE AUTHOR
***

Originally, a New Jersey native, I attended Temple University to major in Elementary Education with concentrations in Theater Arts and Psychology.

Thus, before the books, performance venues, radio opportunities and becoming the PBGP Poetry Slam Champion of 2009, I was a three year old who stood in front of the television with a white and blue laced undershirt with matching blue "Wednesday" Fruit of the Loom underwear singing to Michael Jackson's *"We Are the World"*. *"Put the little meatball on the stage…"* were [and are] the infamous words of my mother and I still live by those words to date. In middle school, I decided to take the work from stage to the page. After striking my notebooks with fragmented thoughts [and horrible spelling], I looked for prospects to perfect the new passion of poetry.

Influenced by my college mentor Dr. Kimmika Williams-Witherspoon, I learned how to shape words to break the Potemkin village of silence and create a voice in the culture of poetry. Excited to share my voice and talents with anyone who will listen, I maintain a home away from home in Philadelphia and New York devoting time to working in the theatre profession, promoting literacy in public schools & art centers, and performing. I'm humbled that the work is taking form in the community. Moreover, I continue scouring the world searching for opportunities to share my dreams with others!

THANK YOU FOR THE CONTINUED SUPPORT!

Confectionately Yours,

TS Hawkins